For P.E.K,
You *are* strong enough x

Timmy and His Two Homes

Written, Edited and Published by Lianne Clancy
Illustrated by Pavani Apsara

Copyright © 2024 Lianne Clancy

All rights reserved. No part of this book may be reproduced in any manner whatsoever without prior written permission of the publisher.

First Printing, 2024

Published by Lianne Clancy
Lianneclancybooks@hotmail.com
@ liannes_literature

Timmy and His Two Homes

Written by
Lianne Clancy

Illustrated by
Pavani Apsara

Hey there,

My name is Timmy and I have a special story to share.

Would you like to hear it?...

Yippee!

This story is all about my family and me.

In my home
There lived my mummy, my daddy, my big brother and me.

I really loved that home we all used to share,

My brother and I had lots of fun playing there.

Although our parents always smiled when we were near,

Our home was often filled with a strange feeling,

And hushed whispers I couldn't quite hear.

Our parents tried their best to show us that everything was fine,

But we were clever boys and understood that,

They just couldn't agree a lot of the time.

As they tucked us into bed each night,

They would kiss our heads and whisper,

'we love you both so very much,
now, close your eyes and sleep tight!'

It was during these times when they thought we were fast asleep,

Down the stairs we would silently creep.
Holding my brother's hand ever so tight,

As we listened to the sounds of a whispered fight.

Early one morning, our parents told us
they had something important to say.

My brother held my hand and I knew
that everything would be okay.

Mummy and daddy told us that things
were going to change;

We were going to have two homes
from now on
And that in the beginning,
it might feel a bit strange.

Our parents don't live in the same
home anymore,

And things *are* quite different
from before.

They still see each other a lot of
the time,

During pick ups and drop offs,
and I can tell
They are both feeling just fine.

They even speak much kinder to each other now.

They don't ever whisper,

They don't ever shout!

Instead of having one strange
feeling home

Where our parents felt like
they had to pretend,

We now have two happy homes
where we live and play,

And everything worked out okay in
the end.

There is one thing that I know will
always stay the same,

And that is how much my parents
love my brother and me!

And because of that love,
I know I will be okay;

No matter where my homes will be.

So, if your story is the same as mine,
Remember; try not to worry too much,
Because everything will be okay in time.

The End.

www.ingramcontent.com/pod-product-compliance
Lightning Source LLC
Chambersburg PA
CBHW041201290426
44109CB00002B/95